HOLIDAY

C as

www.raintreepublishers.co.uk
Visit our website to find out
more information about
Raintree books.

To order:

☎ Phone 0845 6044371

🖷 Fax +44 (0) 1865 312263

✉ Email myorders@raintreepublishers.co.uk

Customers from outside the UK please telephone +44 1865 312262

Raintree is an imprint of Capstone Global Library Limited, a company
incorporated in England and Wales having its registered office at 7 Pilgrim
Street, London, EC4V 6LB – Registered company number: 6695582

Text © Capstone Global Library Limited 2011
First published in hardback in 2011
First published in paperback in 2012

British Library Cataloguing in Publication Data
Dickmann, Nancy.
    Christmas. -- (Holidays and festivals)
    1. Christmas--Pictorial works--Juvenile literature.
    I. Title II. Series
    394.2'663-dc22

Acknowledgements
We would like to thank the following for permission to reproduce
photographs: Alamy pp. **5** (© i love images), **8** (© World Religions Photo
Library), **9** (© LHB Photo), **12**, **20** (© Image Source), **15**, **23 top** (© Adrian
Sherratt), **21** (© Frances Roberts), **23 bottom** (© World Religions Photo
Library); Corbis pp. **6** (© The Gallery Collection), **7** (© Lebrecht Music
& Arts), **19** (© Larry Williams); Getty Images pp. **4** (Thinkstock), **10**, **23
middle** (Yellow Dog Productions/The Image Bank), **11** (Cameron Spencer),
13 (Romeo Gacad/AFP), **16** (Peter Dazeley/Photodisc), **18** (Heinrich van
den Berg); On Asia Images p. **14** (Lu Guang); Shutterstock pp. **17** (©
Monkey Business Images), **22 top left** (© bhathaway), **22 top right** (©
Doremi), **22 bottom left** (© Jurand), **bottom right** (© carballo).

Front cover photograph of nativity scene reproduced with permission of
iStockphoto (© Lisa Thornberg). Back cover photograph reproduced with
permission of Alamy (© Adrian Sherratt).

We would like to thank Diana Bentley, Dee Reid, Nancy Harris, and
Richard Aubrey for their invaluable help in the preparation of this book.

Every effort has been made to contact copyright holders of material
reproduced in this book. Any omissions will be rectified in subsequent
printings if notice is given to the publishers.

Contents

What is a festival?

A festival is a time when people come together to celebrate.

Christian people celebrate Christmas on the 25th of December.

The story of Christmas

Jesus

Long ago, a baby called Jesus was born.

Jesus's parents had nowhere
to stay.

Jesus was born in a stable.

Christian people believe he was the son of God.

Celebrating Christmas today

Christmas is when Christian people celebrate Jesus's birthday.

People celebrate Christmas in different ways.

Some people put up decorations.

Some people have a Christmas tree.

Some people go to church.

Some people sing carols.

Some people send cards.

Some people get together and eat a special meal.

Some people give gifts.

Father Christmas

Some people believe Father Christmas brings them gifts.

Christmas is a time for kindness.

Christmas is a time for giving to others.

Things to look for

Christmas tree

Father Christmas

Jesus

star

Have you seen these things? They make people think of Christmas.

Picture glossary

 **carol** special song that is sung at festivals

 **Christian people** people who follow the teachings of Jesus

 **stable** building where animals live

Index

Notes for parents and teachers

Before reading

Ask the children if they know what holidays and festivals are. Can they name any festivals they celebrate with their families? Talk about birthdays and why they are celebrated. How do they celebrate their own birthday? Christian people, who follow the religion of Christianity celebrate the birth of Jesus at Christmas. Some children from non-Christian or non-religious families may also celebrate Christmas in a secular way.

After reading

• Provide a selection of Christmas cards, both religious and secular. Ask the children to look at the symbols and decorations used. Which aspects of Christmas do they think each one represents? Help the children to design their own Christmas cards.

• Explain that Advent is the period of preparation for the celebration of the birth of Jesus and lasts for about four weeks. The name comes from the Latin 'adventus' which means 'coming'. Talk about ways people celebrate Advent, such as by lighting candles or keeping Advent calendars. Help the children to make an Advent wreath.

• Discuss the idea that some of the most appreciated gifts are not objects but gifts of time and love. Ask the children to think of 'invisible gifts' for their family and friends. Suggest ideas such as sharing a favourite toy, helping out with household chores, or doing a favourite activity together. Help the children make personalized 'gift vouchers' to give to family and friends.